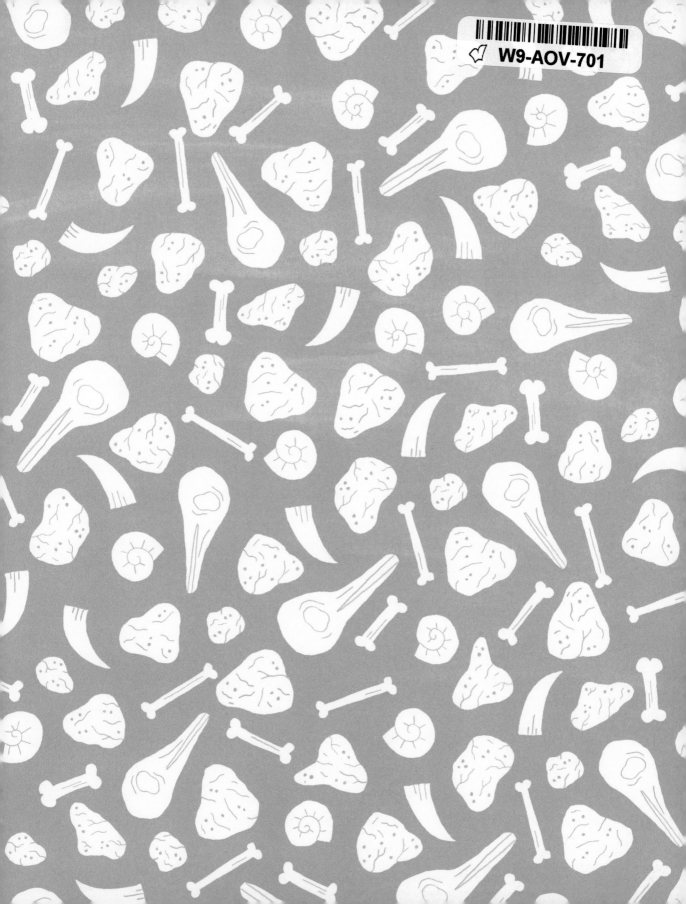

Little People, **BIG DREAMS**™

MARY ANNING

Written by
Maria Isabel Sánchez Vegara

Illustrated by
Popy Matigot

Frances Lincoln
Children's Books

Little Mary was the tenth child of the Annings, a family who lived in a small town on the south coast of England. She was just a baby when a flash of lightning struck an oak tree above her. Miraculously, Mary survived.

Mary's parents were very poor and, from an early age, she was happy to lend a helping hand. She joined her father on dangerous walks to the cliffs looking for shells and bones. One looked like a crocodile's tooth!

Back home, she spent hours cleaning her treasures, hoping to sell some to tourists who visited her town. Soon, everybody knew where to find little Mary— selling seashells by the seashore.

Mary only went to school on Sundays, but it gave her the confidence to learn how to read and write.

One day, after buying one of her curiosities,
a wealthy lady gave her a book that blew her mind.

It turned out that the tooth she had found was not
from a crocodile, but from an animal that had roamed
the Earth millions of years before. This tooth was now a fossil,
and hunting for them became Mary's greatest passion.

When her father became ill and passed away, Mary didn't give up—she continued to hunt for fossils and support the family. Her dog, Tray, was always by her side and they made a perfect team. He loved bones, too!

One morning, she was at the beach with her brother
Joseph when he spotted something in the rocks.
It was a skull bigger than Mary!

She thought more might be hidden in the sand,
and she started digging, day after day.

Mary had discovered the first complete skeleton of a creature that lived in the time of the dinosaurs!

A collector gave her 23 pounds for it, which was more than enough money to buy a whole month of food for her family.

The skeleton was a type of marine reptile called *Ichthyosaurus*, and it ended up on display at the British Museum.

Of course, Mary deserved to go to college, but
at that time, only wealthy men were allowed to do so.
Still, she read all she could about rocks and bones,
taking notes and drawing every fossil she found.

Mary became a true fossil expert all by herself. She discovered the first *Plesiosaurus*, and after she took a closer look at what scientists believed were rare stones, she realized they were... dinosaur poop!

She was always happy to share her knowledge with scientists who visited her, asking for advice. Sadly, some weren't real gentlemen. Many books were written using her discoveries, but no-one ever mentioned her name.

It took almost a lifetime for the Geological Society of London to acknowledge Mary's contributions and offer her membership. Little did she know that, one day, a new species of ichthyosaur would be named after her.

ICHTHYOSAURUS

And little Mary, the Mother of Paleontology, left us
a piece of advice as valuable as her discoveries...
Sometimes people won't recognize your achievements,
but don't worry! Time will place them where they belong.

MARY ANNING

(Born 1799 • Died 1847)

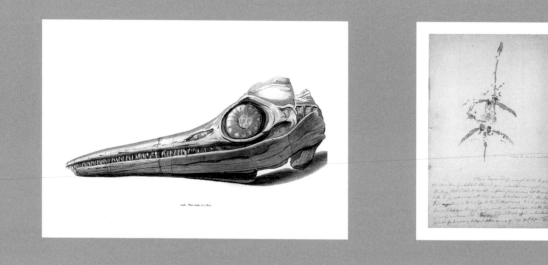

1812   1823

Born on a bright May morning in 1799, Mary Anning was welcomed
into a family of nine children in Lyme Regis, in the southwest English
county of Dorset. Her family were very poor, and Mary's father, Richard,
was a cabinetmaker who collected fossils in his spare time. Aged six,
Mary would join him on his fossil-hunting expeditions, scouring the
beaches surrounding their home. Richard taught his daughter how to
look for and clean fossils, which could then be displayed and sold in his
shop. At the time, fossil hunting was becoming popular among wealthy
Georgians, who were avid collectors and keepers of curiosity cabinets.
Unable to go to school, like many girls of the time, Mary mostly taught
herself to read and write. When she was 11, her father Richard died,

1823   c. 1840

and Mary was encouraged to support the family. A year later, when her brother Joseph found a strange-looking fossilized skull, Mary excavated it and uncovered the outline of its 17 feet-long skeleton. It would go on to be named *Ichthyosaurus*—an extinct marine reptile that lived in the time of the dinosaurs. In 1823, Mary was also the first to discover the complete skeleton of *Plesiosaurus*. But male scientists of the time did not recognize Mary's work, even when writing about her discoveries. In 1828, she dug out the remains of *Pterodactyl*, and went on to pioneer the study of coprolites—or fossilized poo. Until her death, Mary continued to discover fossil after fossil, sparking a wider general interest in paleontology. Today, her discoveries and contributions to science are celebrated around the world.

Want to find out more about **Mary Anning?**

Read these great books:

Mary Anning: The Story of the Great Fossil Hunter by G.D. Waters

Stone Girl, Bone Girl by Laurence Anholt

If you're in Dorset, England, you can also visit the Lyme Regis Museum, where Mary Anning lived!

Brimming with creative inspiration, how-to projects, and useful information to enrich your everyday life, Quarto Knows is a favourite destination for those pursuing their interests and passions. Visit our site and dig deeper with our books into your area of interest: Quarto Creates, Quarto Cooks, Quarto Homes, Quarto Lives, Quarto Drives, Quarto Explores, Quarto Gifts, or Quarto Kids.

Text © 2021 Maria Isabel Sánchez Vegara. Illustrations © Popy Matigot 2021.

Original concept of the series by Maria Isabel Sánchez Vegara, published by Alba Editorial, s.l.u

Produced under trademark licence from Alba Editorial s.l.u and Beautifool Couple S.L.

First Published in the UK in 2021 by Frances Lincoln Children's Books, an imprint of The Quarto Group.

The Old Brewery, 6 Blundell Street, London N7 9BH, United Kingdom.

T 020 7700 6700 **www.QuartoKnows.com**

A catalog record for this book is available from the British Library.

ISBN 978-0-7112-5554-8

Set in Futura BT.

Published by Katie Cotton • Designed by Sasha Moxon

Edited by Katy Flint • Production by Nikki Ingram

Editorial Assistance from Alex Hithersay

Manufactured In China CC122020

1 3 5 7 9 8 6 4 2

Photographic acknowledgements (pages 28-29, from left to right): 1. 1812 – The fossil skull of an ichthyosaur discovered by Joseph Anning and Mary Anning in 1812. Engraving, 1814. © Granger Historical Picture Archive / Alamy Stock Photo. 2. 1823 (letter) – Letter concerning the discovery of Plesiosaurus dinosaur fossil, from Mary Anning, December 26th, 1823 © incamerastock / Alamy Stock Photo. 3. 1823 (photo) – Natural History Museum, Exhibit of Pliosaur Dinosaur Fossil discovered by Mary Anning (1799-1847) © Steve Vidler / Alamy Stock Photo. 4. Ca. 1840 – 'MARY ANNING (1799-1847), English fossil collector and palaeontologist with her dog, Tray. Artist unknown. © Pictorial Press Ltd / Alamy Stock Photo.

Collect the Little People, BIG DREAMS™ series:

FRIDA KAHLO

ISBN: 978-1-84780-783-0

COCO CHANEL

ISBN: 978-1-84780-784-7

MAYA ANGELOU

ISBN: 978-1-84780-889-9

AMELIA EARHART

ISBN: 978-1-84780-888-2

AGATHA CHRISTIE

ISBN: 978-1-84780-960-5

MARIE CURIE

ISBN: 978-1-84780-962-9

ROSA PARKS

ISBN: 978-1-78603-018-4

AUDREY HEPBURN

ISBN: 978-1-78603-053-5

EMMELINE PANKHURST

ISBN: 978-1-78603-020-7

ELLA FITZGERALD

ISBN: 978-1-78603-087-0

ADA LOVELACE

ISBN: 978-1-78603-076-4

JANE AUSTEN

ISBN: 978-1-78603-120-4

GEORGIA O'KEEFFE

ISBN: 978-1-78603-122-8

HARRIET TUBMAN

ISBN: 978-1-78603-227-0

ANNE FRANK

ISBN: 978-1-78603-229-4

MOTHER TERESA

ISBN: 978-1-78603-230-0

JOSEPHINE BAKER

ISBN: 978-1-78603-228-7

L. M. MONTGOMERY

ISBN: 978-1-78603-233-1

JANE GOODALL

ISBN: 978-1-78603-231-7

SIMONE DE BEAUVOIR

ISBN: 978-1-78603-232-4

MUHAMMAD ALI

ISBN: 978-1-78603-331-4

STEPHEN HAWKING

ISBN: 978-1-78603-333-8

MARIA MONTESSORI

ISBN: 978-1-78603-755-8

VIVIENNE WESTWOOD

ISBN: 978-1-78603-757-2

MAHATMA GANDHI

ISBN: 978-1-78603-787-9

DAVID BOWIE

ISBN: 978-1-78603-332-1

WILMA RUDOLPH

ISBN: 978-1-78603-751-0

DOLLY PARTON

ISBN: 978-1-78603-760-2

BRUCE LEE

ISBN: 978-1-78603-789-3

RUDOLF NUREYEV

ISBN: 978-1-78603-791-6

ZAHA HADID

ISBN: 978-1-78603-745-9

MARY SHELLEY

ISBN: 978-1-78603-748-0

MARTIN LUTHER KING JR.

ISBN: 978-0-7112-4567-9

DAVID ATTENBOROUGH

ISBN: 978-0-7112-4564-8

ASTRID LINDGREN

ISBN: 978-0-7112-5217-2

EVONNE GOOLAGONG

ISBN: 978-0-7112-4586-0

BOB DYLAN

ISBN: 978-0-7112-4675-1

ALAN TURING

ISBN: 978-0-7112-4678-2

BILLIE JEAN KING

ISBN: 978-0-7112-4693-5

GRETA THUNBERG

ISBN: 978-0-7112-5645-3

JESSE OWENS

ISBN: 978-0-7112-4583-9

JEAN-MICHEL BASQUIAT

ISBN: 978-0-7112-4580-8

ARETHA FRANKLIN

ISBN: 978-0-7112-4686-7

CORAZON AQUINO

ISBN: 978-0-7112-4684-3

PELÉ

ISBN: 978-0-7112-4573-0

ERNEST SHACKLETON

ISBN: 978-0-7112-4571-6

STEVE JOBS

ISBN: 978-0-7112-4577-8

AYRTON SENNA

ISBN: 978-0-7112-4672-0

LOUISE BOURGEOIS

ISBN: 978-0-7112-4690-4

ELTON JOHN

ISBN: 978-0-7112-5840-2

JOHN LENNON

ISBN: 978-0-7112-5767-2

PRINCE

ISBN: 978-0-7112-5439-8

CHARLES DARWIN

ISBN: 978-0-7112-5771-9

CAPTAIN TOM MOORE

ISBN: 978-0-7112-6209-6

HANS CHRISTIAN ANDERSEN

ISBN: 978-0-7112-5934-8

STEVIE WONDER

ISBN: 978-0-7112-5775-7

MEGAN RAPINOE

ISBN: 978-0-7112-5783-2

MARY ANNING

ISBN: 978-0-7112-5554-8

MALALA YOUSAFZAI

ISBN: 978-0-7112-5904-1

ACTIVITY BOOKS

STICKER ACTIVITY BOOK

ISBN: 978-0-7112-6012-2

COLORING BOOK

ISBN: 978-0-7112-6136-5

LITTLE ME, BIG DREAMS JOURNAL

ISBN: 978-0-7112-4889-2

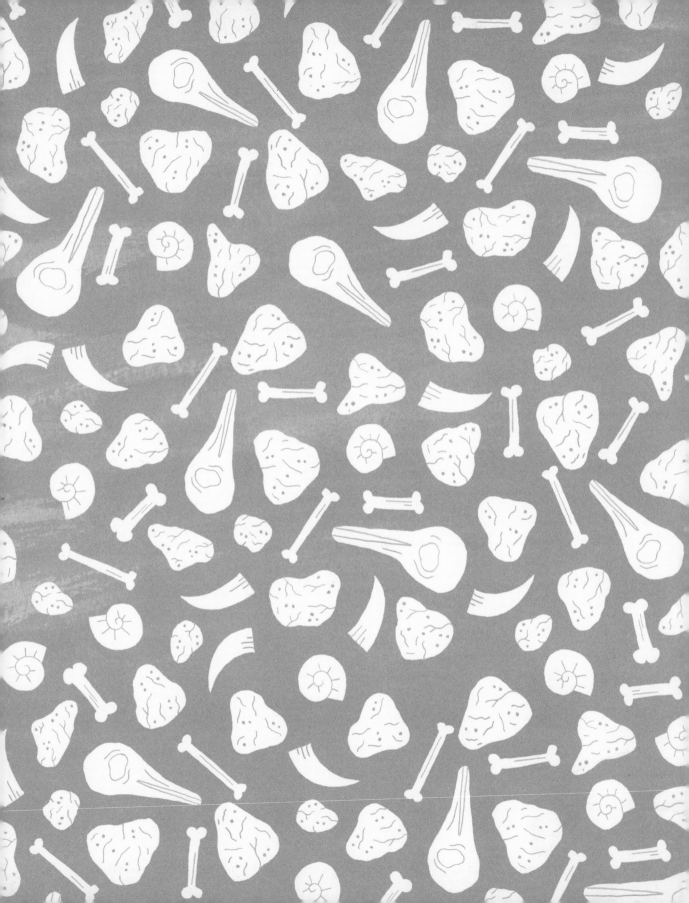